HOW TO PLAY LIKE A PRO

HOCKEY SKILLS

BY JAMES MacDONALD

Enslow Elementary

an imprint of

Enslow Publishers, Inc.

40 Industrial Road
Box 398
Berkeley Heights, NJ 07922
USA

http://www.enslow.com

Enslow Elementary, an imprint of Enslow Publishers, Inc.

Enslow Elementary® is a registered trademark of Enslow Publishers, Inc.

Library of Congress Cataloging-in-Publication Data
MacDonald, James, 1971 Oct. 8-
  Hockey skills : how to play like a pro / James MacDonald.
     p. cm. — (How to play like a pro)
  Summary: "Learn how to skate, shoot, handle the puck and tend the goal like the professionals"—Provided by publisher.
  Includes bibliographical references and index.
  ISBN-13: 978-0-7660-3207-1
  1. Hockey—Juvenile literature. I. Title.
  GV847.25.M33 2009
  796.962'2—dc22

                              2007048517

Credits
Editorial Direction: Red Line Editorial, Inc.
Cover & interior design: Becky Daum
Editors: Bob Temple, Dave McMahon
Special thanks to Jeff Sauer, former head coach at the University of Wisconsin, for his help with this book.

Printed in the United States of America

10 9 8 7 6 5 4 3 2 1

Photo credits: AP/Jacques Boissinot, 1, 19; AP Photo/The Columbian, Steven Lane, 4; AP/Kathy Willens, 7; 123rf/Joseph Gareri, 8; AP/Ann Heisenfelt, 9; iStockPhoto/James Boulette, 10; AP/Rusty Kennedy, 11; AP/Anders Wiklund, 12; AP/Gene J. Puskar, 13; Dreamstime/Iofoto, 14, 34; AP Photo/Christof Stach, 15; AP/Mark Avery, 17; AP/LM Otero, 18; AP Photo/Michael Tweed, 20; iStockPhoto/Walik, 21, 23, 28, 31; AP/Danny Moloshok, 22; iStockPhoto/Joseph Gareri, 24, 40, 44; AP/Jim Mone, 25; AP/Mark Avery, 27; AP/Gene J. Puskar, 29; AP/Paul Sancya, 30; Dreamstime/Joseph Gareri, 32; AP/Bill Kostroun, 33; AP/John Woods, 35; AP/Chuck Stoody, 37; Dreamstime/Kathy Wynn, 38; AP/Andy King, 39; AP/Matt Slocum, 41; AP/Jeff Lewis, 42; iStockPhoto/Jami Garrison, 43; AP/Rudi Blaha, 45.

Cover Photo: Sam Gagner, son of former NHL player Dave Gagner, practices at a hockey camp in 2007. He was later drafted in the first round of the NHL draft by the Edmonton Oilers (AP/Jacques Boissinot). Inset: Mike Modano (9) of the Dallas Stars eludes a defender (AP/LM Otero).

CONTENTS

Hockey is a fast-paced, intense game that requires practice and skill. Players who are just starting to learn the game are as important to the team as those players with experience. The sport requires teamwork and sportsmanship from all players in order to make it enjoyable.

One of the best things about hockey is that it's for male and female players, young and old. Some hockey players begin playing at age three, and enjoy it so much that they continue to play into their seventies.

Safety is important at every level of hockey. Hockey players should always wear a helmet when they are on the ice, and young players should always make sure an adult is nearby. The tips and drills provided in this book are always meant to be played when wearing a helmet—full equipment is recommended—and with a coach or adult at the rink.

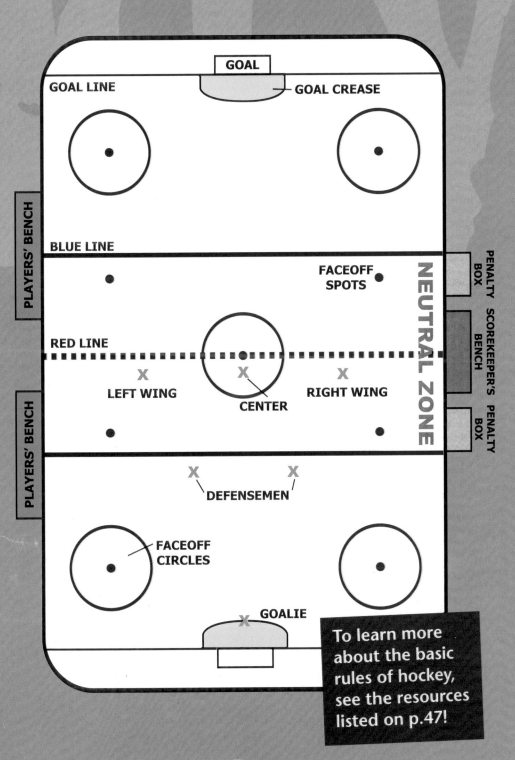

GOAL

GOAL LINE

GOAL CREASE

PLAYERS' BENCH

BLUE LINE

FACEOFF SPOTS

NEUTRAL ZONE

PENALTY BOX

SCOREKEEPER'S BENCH

RED LINE

LEFT WING

CENTER

RIGHT WING

PENALTY BOX

PLAYERS' BENCH

DEFENSEMEN

FACEOFF CIRCLES

GOALIE

To learn more about the basic rules of hockey, see the resources listed on p.47!

SKATING

Without skating, it isn't ice hockey! Skating is the first building block of hockey and gives the sport its speed, action, and constant motion. Thanks to skating, there is always something happening on the ice, even when players don't have the puck or aren't involved in the play. Players need to keep their heads up at all times.

Hockey players can zip much more quickly around the ice than players in other sports. As a player becomes a faster skater, hockey becomes one of the most exciting games in the world.

For players of any age, the most important element in skating is balance. New skaters tend to stand up straight on their skates, but it is better to stay low.

Have Fun Skating

Learn to skate first, then try to pick up other hockey skills. There are many elements to hockey, but they all begin with skating. That's a good thing, too, because skating can be the most fun of them all.

It is very important for a player to find a comfortable skate. Skates should be a half- to full-size smaller than the player's shoe size.

Lift Those Skates

Beginning skaters tend to keep their skates close to the ice. The skater's goal is to lift the skates and allow them to move independently.

In 2007, Sidney Crosby (87) of the Pittsburgh Penguins became the youngest player ever to win the Hart Trophy, as the NHL's most valuable player. He was only 19!

Speedsters

As adults, many players can reach speeds of 30 mph.

Skating begins with the start. The idea is to transition from a "ready position" into an effective skating stride. In the ready position, the knees are slightly bent and the player leans forward.

With the most basic start, the player faces forward and pushes off the foot of his or her choice. That's the "back" skate, and it provides the power. The "front" skate provides support and steering. With each stride, each skate's role changes.

The Crossover Start

Rather than moving forward from "ready," a player looks over his or her shoulder and leans left or right. The rear skate is lifted and pulled over the front skate. The weight transfers, the shoulders swing around, and the skate lands.

The "back" skate provides power during the "start."

Gaining Speed

Starts are important no matter where players are on the ice. Even when gliding, the start technique is used to pick up speed again.

Long strides are strong strides.

Fast Marian

More than 25 percent of NHL players in a 2007 ESPN poll thought Minnesota Wild forward Marian Gaborik (10) was their league's fastest player.

The thigh presses the knee down. The inside edge of the skate blade digs in and pushes for more speed.

"Front" skate.

Skaters who crouch down will generate the most power with a 90-degree angle at the knee.

"Back" skate.

One of hockey's most valuable skills is the stop, and not just to keep a player from an unwelcome meeting with the boards.

Hockey is a constantly changing game. The puck reverses direction. Offense becomes defense. Then defense becomes offense. And it happens faster than players can move. The better a player is at stopping and starting, the more often he or she will be part of the action.

T-Stop

T-stops are a great way for a player to become comfortable on one edge. The front skate points the toe forward. The heel points into the arch of the rear skate. The rear skate faces sideways to form the T. The player simply leans back and lets the rear skate blade do most of the work.

The hockey stop takes practice but is quite worth the effort. When a player can stop this way on both sides, he or she has added an invaluable and lifelong skill.

The first stop most players learn is called the snowplow. Players slow to a stop by bending their knees forward, pushing their heels out and pointing their toes inward.

Simon Gagne (12) of the NHL's Philadelphia Flyers is a two-time Olympian for Canada.

The player uses his or her knee-bend to slow the body.

The fastest stop is the quick and powerful "hockey stop." It uses an edge of both skates at the same time. The edges dig into the ice, slide a bit, grab more ice, and create enough resistance to put on the brakes. A fun part of the technique is to turn up a cloud of snow.

Edges dig into the ice.

Some new to the sport may not even be aware that a pair of skates not only has "edges," but four of them. Both the left and right skate have inside and outside edges.

When a player stands on his or her skates, most likely they won't be able to feel all four edges. As soon as they want to move, however, those edges are doing all the work.

Conquering the idea of edges allows skaters to become more confident. The next step is to begin cornering, or turning quickly, and adding crossovers. Once a player can corner hard and cross one skate over the other, he or she will be able to skate with more agility and speed in any direction.

Practice

Executing crossovers while skating around a faceoff circle located to the left or right of either goal crease is a popular drill. This teaches technique, balance, edges, and—most important—acceleration.

A Thin Line

Blades on ice hockey skates are approximately one-eighth of an inch wide.

When a player crosses over to the right, he or she is on the outside edge of the right skate and the inside edge of the left skate. The reverse is true for turning left.

Star Power

Veteran Jaromir Jagr (68) entered the NHL in 1990 and led the league in scoring five times through 2006–07. Here, he's shown playing for the Czech Republic at the 2006 Winter Olympic Games.

Crossing over allows a player to accelerate and change direction at the same time.

The player should control the skates, not the other way around.

SKATING BACKWARD

Some believe skating backward is for defensemen only. That is not true. Defensemen spend more of their time skating backward, but forwards at all levels are better off learning early, too.

If a player is forced to catch up to a play, he or she may "backcheck" to catch up. The defensive player can then pivot into skating backward if the play calls for it. For forwards and defensemen, the goal is to transfer from forward to backward as quickly as possible. This makes for a versatile player who can move with the play.

Like skating forward, the foundation is balance and a sturdy ready position.

Backchecking occurs when forwards defend the approaching wingers all the way down the ice in order to prevent strong passes to the wingers.

Practice

Execute crossovers while skating backward. This is the fastest way to pick up speed. It takes many hours of practice to become effective at doing backward crossovers.

Getting Started

To start moving backward, players carve a crescent shape in the ice with one skate—pushing one skate out and drawing a semi-circle with the inside edge. The other skate supports the body. Once in motion, the player repeats the crescent with the inside edge of the other skate.

Offensive players have to react quickly to strong backward skaters.

In addition to the crescent cuts, players can maintain speed by wiggling both skates under the body. This creates two parallel tracks of S-curves in the ice.

Bend at the knees and waist to keep your balance.

Skates carve crescents, or C-cuts.

STICKHANDLING

Hockey is thrilling to play, even when a player does not have the puck on his or her stick. But players can really start to enjoy the game as they learn how to handle the puck better.

There's only one puck to be shared between many skaters, so each of them has to make the most of his or her time with it. Good sports are always willing to pass the puck.

The better a player is at handling the puck, the more valuable that player is. The best way to do that is to practice. And practice. Then practice some more.

Players who are most comfortable with the puck—especially moving it quickly from forehand to backhand—have the most success.

Score a Goal

The idea of competitive hockey is to move the puck around the ice and into a position to score goals. That starts with individuals handling the puck. Players who know how to handle the puck are on their way to becoming goal-scorers.

Players can practice stickhandling by using a small ball. Set up an obstacle course on the sidewalk or driveway to move around in

Use the Blade

The best puck-handlers in the world can pull the puck left and right, forward and backward. They use both sides of the stick's blade—and they can do it all at top speed.

Players rarely touch the puck during a game—well under a minute total in a youth game.

Carrying the puck close to the body gives a player more options and keeps it away from defenders.

Ryan Getzlaf (15) won a Stanley Cup in his second season with the Anaheim Ducks. As a center, he's relied on to skate with the puck, all while looking to pass it to teammates.

Eventually, a player learns to roll his or her wrists to cradle the puck. This provides even more control.

He's No. 1

Michigan-born Mike Modano (9) was the top pick in the 1988 NHL draft. He has played his entire career with the same franchise—the Minnesota North Stars and Dallas Stars. He scored his 500th NHL goal in 2006–07 and has more career points than any other U.S.-born player.

Sticks come in all shapes and sizes, so players choose the length and curve they find most comfortable.

The most important tool in stickhandling is the stick. At the bottom is the blade. It has a forehand (front) side and a backhand side. A right-handed player will hold the stick with his or her right hand lower and left hand higher. It's the opposite for left-handed players. Either way, the top hand operates the blade of the stick.

The best players are able to use both the forehand and backhand early. Keeping control of the puck is achieved by sliding it from one blade side, catching with the other, and then sliding it back.

Steer the Puck

The top hand is the most important part in stickhandling. At any age, it's important to remember that the top hand can steer the stick blade more quickly than the bottom hand. Players who can steer the puck while looking ahead have an advantage.

Eyes on target. →

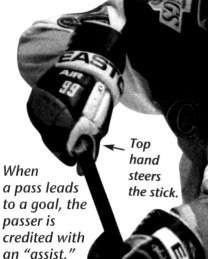

Passing Fancy

Once a player masters this sweeping motion, he or she can add the "saucer" pass. A player lifts the puck off the ice but keeps the puck parallel to the ice so that it can land flat. This helps make passes over a defender's stick.

← Top hand steers the stick.

When a pass leads to a goal, the passer is credited with an "assist."

The Great One

Wayne Gretzky scored more goals than any player in NHL history. But he was also known for his amazing passing skills. He had 1,963 assists in 1,487 regular-season games.

Stick continues to move forward after puck is passed.

Another way to avoid a defender is to bounce the puck off the boards.

TICKHANDLING

PASSING

The passing game adds another dimension to hockey. Once two players can trade the puck, they are much more effective. When three, four, or all five skaters can move the puck around, they are primed for success.

Good passing starts with the passer's head up. The goal is to see as much of the ice as possible. Once the player decides to pass, he or she sweeps the stick in the direction of the target and follows through.

At higher levels, the passer aims the puck where the receiver will be, not where he or she is at the moment of the pass.

Players who know how to pass as soon as they receive the puck are able to create open shots for their teammates.

Smooth Pass

In the easiest pass, the puck is swept from behind the back skate. The wrists turn to slide the stick. As part of this motion, the stick blade follows through smoothly. Having the puck too far ahead of the back skate makes the pass more difficult.

RECEIVING

Every pass needs a target. And, just like good passing, good receiving begins with the head up. Always be ready for a pass.

Once the puck has left the passer's stick, the receiver bends slightly at the waist and keeps the knees bent. It is very important to keep the stick on the ice so that the puck does not slide underneath it. The stick also provides a target for the passer.

Cradle the Puck

The principle is the same for receiving a pass on the backhand: make eye-contact, provide a target, and prepare for the puck. Cradle a hard pass by moving the stick backward slightly as the puck hits the blade.

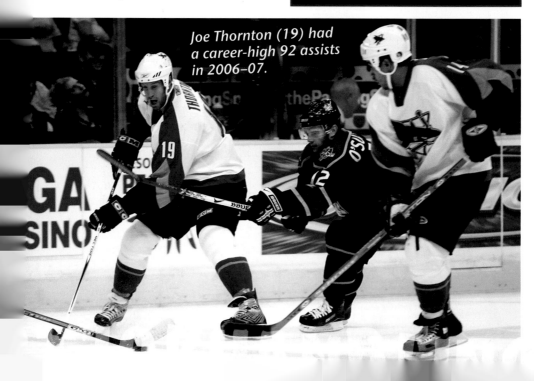

Joe Thornton (19) had a career-high 92 assists in 2006–07.

Without talking, players can communicate their interest in receiving a pass. When a passer or receiver looks up, they can see their options. Talking, of course, does help, but it can be difficult with a mouthpiece in place.

Be a Target

Players move to different parts of the ice to "get open" for a pass. The better receivers keep their stick on the ice and show passers a target, too.

Slap the stick on the ice to signal a passing target.

Cradle the puck by moving the stick back slightly as the puck arrives.

Players should not stand still while waiting for the puck. Instead, they may pick up speed, prepare, then receive the puck on the move.

MOVING

Hockey skills such as skating, passing, and shooting are just starting points of the sport.

When all of these skills are put into motion, the game of hockey really comes alive. Stickhandling through the defense creates excitement.

Looking for an offensive chance against a player who has stopped or pivoted is another way to become part of the game. In hockey, the more movement, the better for your team.

As players progress, the gaps between these activities close. Starting and stopping, backhand and forehand, and crossovers and pivots all become natural to hockey players. And this is why so many love the game.

Practice

Try doing all of these skills at once: skate backward and stickhandle with forehand and backhand. Cross over one way, then pivot and cross in the other direction. Do it with a puck and make a pass, or try to score.

Keep the puck away from your opponent.

Even at its highest levels, hockey is based on the skills players learn very early.

Top players can handle the puck at full speed around, in front of, or behind their bodies.

To pick up speed while racing to get the puck, players take the bottom hand off their sticks and pump their arms.

Get Creative

Stickhandling while moving forward gives a player his or her best options. While crossing over or carving a turn, the ice can be opened up to new passing angles. It can also set up the "deke" move.

SHOOTING

Hockey is a game of puck control, but there is one time to let it go—when it's time to shoot at the goal. Shots come in almost as many variations as the players who take them.

Some say every shot is a good one. Others suggest waiting for the goalie to leave a spot open before shooting at the net. Either way, it is important to remember that the shooter is always trying to score a goal . . . even if it means setting up a rebound.

The best places to aim are generally the corners of the net, between a goaltender's skates, and under his or her arms. Often, the most effective shot is not the hardest but the one that is placed accurately. Developing an accurate shot leads to success.

Quick Release

One of the keys to a good shot is a "quick release." That just means a player can shoot the puck without giving a goalie much time to wonder where it might be going.

A typical player takes only a few shots per game. Practicing away from game situations becomes very important for aspiring

Be Patient

Sometimes, waiting for a goalie to move may open up a hole that wouldn't be there with a forced shot.

A player is almost always moving before a shot, so practice shooting at the goal from different angles.

Some top players grew up shooting hundreds of pucks a day to improve their shooting skills.

From 2001–2007, the Calgary Flames' Jarome Iginla (left) averaged more than 40 goals per season. He was named the team's captain in 2003.

WRIST SHOT

Of all the shots, the wrist shot is considered the most accurate and most effective. It can be learned at a young age and developed as a player grows older. By the time an adult player is taking wrist shots, the shot probably remains the most often used.

Take a wrist shot by placing the bottom hand down the stick shaft. The blade should come behind the leg that's furthest away from the target. The bottom hand provides the power. Flick the wrist as the puck is swept forward.

Even the motion is straightforward. A player takes the sweeping move of a pass and aims it toward the net. Players who incorporate a leg drive will make the shot faster.

Hit Your Spots

After gaining familiarity with the motion of a wrist shot, aiming pucks at different parts of a net is time well spent—even if it's not on the ice. The more practice shots a player takes, the more accurate his or her shots will be.

Advanced players lean into their sticks. The resulting stick bend provides a whipping action and extra pace on a shot.

The best place to start a wrist shot is from a spot behind the back skate, so the arms can fire across the front of the body.

Amazing Ovechkin

Alexander Ovechkin (8) was named the NHL's top rookie for 2005–06. In 2006–07, he scored 46 goals.

Once a player can lift the puck, he or she has even more options and places to score goals.

Because the shot requires such a quick release, it can be harder for a goaltender to read where a snap shot is going. At the same time, it is difficult to aim a snap shot.

Dazzling Datsyuk

Detroit Red Wings forward Pavel Datsyuk displays the timing technique. He steps into the shot without having full control of the puck, leans on the stick and snaps his wrists through the contact point.

Lean on the stick.

This is a powerful motion and also finishes with a follow-through.

The blade is the part of the stick that hits the puck.

Sweet Spot

A blade's sweet spot is the place on it where the puck receives the most energy from the shooter.

Almost all snap shots need exact timing between the snapping action in the hands and the location of the puck on the blade.

SNAP SHOT

Snap shots are not as accurate as wrist shots. The wrists roll back and snap quickly on a snap shot. Keep the tip of the blade on the ice. The puck needs to be near the front foot. Transfer the weight to the front foot to create power. Follow through by having the stick facing downward.

Snap shots require almost no backswing, and almost zero time. What they do require is lots of practice.

Get There First

The snap shot is especially effective during the rare time a puck is sitting free in front of the net. If a player can jump to the puck and snap that shot before anyone else can collect it, he or she has a better chance of scoring.

Remember, aim for one of the corners of the net.

The Deke Move

A deke, or fake, draws the goaltender far to one side. The shooter tries to make the goaltender believe he's going to take a forehand shot, but pulls it back to his backhand at the last second. In higher levels, this might require quite a bit of stickhandling.

The backhand shot can also be swept off the ice. A player can learn to shoot with the same angles—high to the left and right or under the crossbar—as on the forehand side.

Shooting situations can be tense. The best shooters can relax and make the best shot without stress. Shooters who remember that the backhand shot is an option have a better chance of scoring.

BACKHAND

In shooting opportunities, it is often forgotten that there are two sides of the stick blade. Players favor using the forehand because it feels natural and seems like the quickest way to score.

Besides that, pulling a shot across the body in the other direction can be awkward at first. The more often backhand shots are practiced, the more comfortable players become. A player can become a scoring machine by practicing his or her backhand shot. Backhand shots are often thought of as the hardest to read by a goaltender.

The player who adds a backhand shot adds another element of scoring to his or her game. It also brings the "deke" into play.

REBOUNDS

Because pucks are often lost in the scuffling and shuffling in front of the net, goalies have a hard time keeping their eyes on them in a scramble. And that's why some players make a living scoring on loose pucks near the net.

A player who gets position in front of the net can often get a tip-in goal. These goals occur when the puck bounces off a goalie's pads or stick and lands slightly in front of the net.

Rebound Goals

Players also create their own rebounds. By forcing a goalie to make a difficult save, the shooter can prepare to score on a rebound.

Stick on the Ice

As with any potential scoring situation, a goal-scorer's stick is close enough to the ice to make sure he or she can strike if the puck becomes available.

Hockey Sense

Players who score on rebounds know the game. They watch and remember where pucks wind up after shots. After a while, they'll shoot from those spots— and possibly score.

The best place to cash in on rebounds is in "the slot" and to the sides of the net while facing it. The slot is the area in front of the net.

GOALTENDING

Goaltending can be a lonely job. It can also be very challenging, both physically and mentally. And, it's hot under that equipment! Goaltenders wait for the action to come to them. Who would want to stand in the way of a speeding slap shot?

Well, when that action does arrive, how a goaltender reacts can totally change the game. And that's why some players want to be goaltenders.

Goaltenders are more likely to affect games than any other player on the ice. Some athletes do not want that pressure. Others invite it.

A goaltender's job seems simple—stop the puck. But their impact is so much greater than just making saves.

Head in the Game

Some goaltenders play the puck well enough to be able to pass it to their defensemen. And most give strategy tips to their teammates on the ice.

While skaters play only parts of the game in shifts, goaltenders are on the ice for the entire game. Sometimes, a coach will take a goalie who is not playing well out of the game.

36

Forget Goals

One of the most difficult aspects of goaltending is bouncing back after allowing a goal. It's important to get ready for the game to continue so that you'll be more prepared to stop the next one.

Smart goaltenders like Roberto Luongo (below) follow the play with their eyes and body. Stopping more than 90 percent of shots is considered very good. Through nearly 500 career NHL regular-season games, Luongo has a save percentage of .919.

The average NHL goaltender faces around 25–30 shots per game.

EQUIPMENT

A goaltender is easy to spot. He or she is the one with the huge hockey bag going into the rink. Goaltenders don't wear all that much more than skaters do. But what they do wear is bigger.

Their leg pads are longer, heavier and wider. Their skates have a different look and feel. They wear one special glove to swallow pucks like a baseball mitt and another to hold the stick. Even their sticks and helmets are different.

With skaters, equipment such as helmets, shoulder pads and shin guards is more about safety than function. With goaltenders, equipment is just as much about making saves. Goaltenders are able to remain steady in their positions because they know they will not easily get hurt.

Padding Power

A goaltender's equipment is designed to stop a puck from the front. Padding is far less protective on the goaltender's back. At higher levels, goaltenders wear larger pants with more padding than skaters. Pro leagues limit the size of some pads.

All good goaltenders know how each piece of equipment can help them to stop a shot.

Under the jersey, there is a large chest protector. The chest protector also covers the shoulders.

Catching glove

Leg pads are worn to make saves below the waist.

The blades of a goaltender's skates allow him or her to step side-to-side more easily. The blades are flatter and wider.

STANCE

A goaltender's ready position is slightly different than a skater's ready position. Both positions require that the knees be bent with a forward lean. But a goaltender keeps his or her arms ready to make a save.

The glove hand is open to catch. The blocker hand holds the stick with the blade covering the skates and the arm just off to the side.

Goalies use the crescent to cut back and forth in front of the net.

Stay Sturdy

Goaltenders keep their feet under them and hold their balance on their skates in the ready position. Even something as simple as a sturdy stance can be intimidating to shooters.

Energy Savers

With a proper stance, goaltenders can let many pucks come to them. The less energy used to make a save, the more energy maintained throughout a game.

Younger players may cover less of the net, but younger shooters have more trouble finding those holes. At the youth level, it's an even trade-off.

Square Up

Placement in the crease is important. Goaltenders want to be "square to the shooter." This means facing the shooter with both shoulders and hips.

Deflect high shots with the blocker.

Knees turned inward to close any gaps that the puck could fit through.

When standing, a goaltender isn't only standing. He or she is also following the play and preparing to move.

A goaltender makes life less complicated by reading the play and moving into position.

Goaltenders practice lateral movement by sliding from post to post on their skates.

J.S. Giguere (above) guided the Anaheim Ducks to the NHL Stanley Cup title in 2006–07.

To move in and out of the crease, goaltenders rely on their inside edges. They push their blades out to start the movement, then pull them back in to stop it.

MOVEMENT

Goaltenders can be some of the better skaters on their teams. Goaltending began as a stationary position. No more. The position is now a very athletic one. Goaltenders practice skating, and it is important to be able to move in the crease.

Movement as a goaltender can be achieved in several ways. Lateral movement, from side to side, allows goaltenders to cover both sides of the net. Telescoping, moving in and out from the goal line to the top of the crease, also is done to prevent goals.

Goaltenders need quick reflexes and strong leg muscles to help them pop back into the ready position.

Always cover the post.

Practice

One of the most common drills in goaltending is to drop from a ready position to the knees. Then the goaltender pops back up, all while keeping his or her arms in position, ready to stop the puck. Then it's more ups and downs!

The top priority for any goaltender is to make saves. It's a simple approach, but one that can change the entire flow of a game. In fact, the goalie can even stop the game by "freezing" the puck.

When the goalie puts his or her glove on top of a puck on the ice, covers the puck with his or her body, or catches the puck with his or her glove, the game is stopped. A faceoff, in which an official drops the puck between one player from each team in the circles near the goaltender, allows the game to be restarted.

Shake It Off

Goals happen in hockey. There's no reason to be discouraged when a goal is scored, especially at younger ages. Hockey is an exciting game, and goaltending is just a position in the game. No goaltender stops every shot.

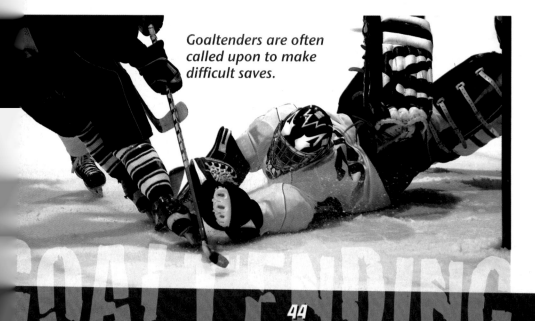

Goaltenders are often called upon to make difficult saves.

Top goaltenders try to have more patience than the shooter. Without committing to a save, he or she can react more quickly to the shot when it finally comes.

No Rebounds

All goaltenders are careful to control rebounds. Some shooters are so good that this becomes difficult.

If the shot can't be controlled, goaltenders try to sweep the puck away from the net and back to teammates to put the puck back in play.

When goaltenders move toward the shooter, the shooter sees less of the net.

★ **assist**—The point awarded to the player or players (two at most) whose pass led to a goal.

★ **backhand**—The back side of a player's stick blade; or a pass or shot performed with that side of the stick.

★ **breakaway**—Any time a player skates to face the goaltender with no defender to stop him or her.

★ **crease**—The area of the ice in front of a goaltender's net.

★ **deke**—To fake a move one way and quickly turn in the other direction.

★ **defenseman**—A player who tries to keep an opposing player from getting into scoring position.

★ **forehand**—The front side of the stick blade; or a pass or shot performed with that side of the stick.

★ **forward**—A player who controls the puck and attempts to get into position to score.

★ **goaltender**—The player responsible for covering his or her team's net and preventing other teams from scoring.

★ **puck-handling**—The act of moving a puck with the stick across the ice. Also known as "stickhandling."

★ **ready position**—A stance with slight bends at the knees and waist. The knees are above the skates and the shoulders are in line with the knees.

★ **save**—When a goaltender stops the shot of an opposing player.

★ **slot**—The area in front of the net, extending out from the crease and between the offensive faceoff circles.

LEARN MORE

INTERNET ADDRESSES

★ **Bertagna Goalie Schools**
   http://www.bertagnagoaltending.com

★ **Hockey Canada**
   http://www.hockeycanada.ca

★ **NHL Kids**
   http://www.nhl.com/kids/index.html

★ **The Science of Hockey**
   http://www.exploratorium.edu/hockey/

★ **USA Hockey**
   http://usahockey.com

BOOKS

★ **Hockey: How to Play Like the Pros,** by Paul Carson and Sean Rossiter. Vancouver, BC: Greystone Books, 2004.

★ **Hockey For Dummies, 2nd Edition,** by John Davidson with John Steinbreder, foreword by Wayne Gretzky, preface by Mike Myers. Indianapolis, IN: Wiley Publishing, Inc., 2001.

★ **Hockey Goaltending: Skills for Ice and In-Line Hockey,** by Brian Daccord, foreword by Martin Brodeur. Champaign, IL: Human Kinetics, 1998.